Lean Startup

*How to Apply the Lean Startup
Methodology to Create, Innovate, and
Accelerate Successful Businesses*

Lean Startup

Table of Contents

Introduction

This book "*Lean Startup: How to Apply the Lean Startup Methodology to Innovate, Accelerate, and Create Successful Businesses*" is a foundational must-read for entrepreneurs. It contains helpful tips on how to create successful businesses using the lean startup methodology. It aims to teach entrepreneurs, both new and seasoned, business innovations fit for the twenty-first century.

Most entrepreneurs fail because they can't follow through with ideas that produce successful and sustainable results. However, the contents of this book will teach entrepreneurs, aspiring entrepreneurs, and even those who are just curious about the whole idea of entrepreneurship. Among these is how to avoid mistakes that can break their business, as well as how to employ validated learning to make their business.

It contains innovative steps, as well as strategies, to help entrepreneurs create and manage their own startup while leveraging on the successes and failures of other entrepreneurs before them. Think of this book as a cookbook for entrepreneurship and management.

Thanks for purchasing this book, I hope you enjoy it!

SECTION 1: Create

Have you ever been in a situation where you have everything down pat in your mind, but these all scatter in all directions as soon as you try to implement them? Well, I have, and believe me, it's not funny. That's why I decided to divide this book into three sections – Create, Innovate, and Accelerate.

In this first section, "Create", I will try to show you everything I know about entrepreneurship and entrepreneurial management. Here, I will identify what an entrepreneur is, what he is made of, and what entrepreneurial management means. I will also try to share some learnings that will determine whether a business is progressing towards its goals or if a bit of science is necessary to make it more sustainable.

Chapter 1: What Makes an Entrepreneur?

Let's start off by defining what an entrepreneur is. In the simplest of explanations, an entrepreneur is someone who is brave enough to set up a business and actually take responsibility for it. That includes welcoming the risks that come with starting a business, embracing those risks, and managing them.

I should know, because I am an entrepreneur, too. I've had years of experience in the field of entrepreneurship, and as such, I can confidently say that over the years, I have learned how to be insightful when it comes to opportunities and threats that are ever-present in this field. Moreover, I have learned how to acclimate, so to speak, with regards to the volatile business and financial climates.

What, though, of new entrepreneurs? Given the fact that they are barely starting, it's safe to say they lack the experience necessary to brave the storm. Yes, they may be risk takers who know how to calculate risks by being level-headed and using good judgment. Nevertheless, there are times when safety guarantees just don't cut it and sure wins are beyond attainable. Believe me when I say these are unavoidable. I have been there, and I have done that. What did I do then? I trusted my gut feelings and decided to brave it and tread on dangerous grounds.

This early, you're probably thinking, "Did this guy even succeed seeing as how he made asinine decisions?" Well, I hope I am not raining on your parade when I say, "I did! I succeeded." However, it was not without difficulties and plenty of uncertainties. Because I chose to be an entrepreneur, I had to be a swift decision-maker who is generally confident with his choices.

Along the way, I learned how to take sides once I've analyzed what is at stake or once I am convinced of the rewards awaiting me despite the risks I had to take. I surmised that I am no fence-sitter, but instead, I can act and decide quickly as long as I have analyzed things and have deduced that positive results will outweigh the risks.

Yes, I don't pretty much believe in luck nor do I believe that I was destined to be a successful entrepreneur from the get-go. Rather, I believe in hard work. I believe that when you create a business from the ground up, you need to plan and predict possible outcomes instead of leaving things to chance. There is no room for compulsiveness when you're an entrepreneur because chances are you will find it difficult to control your ideas, so much so that parts of your life that are separate from your business are disrupted (Farbrot, 2014).

If you truly want to succeed as an entrepreneur, you need to realize, just as I did, that there is no substitute for hard work. In a startup business, which is pretty much what new entrepreneurs have in their hands, you need to follow a grinding work schedule that allows you to be all over several places at one time. "Huh," you're probably thinking, "does this mean I need to clone myself?" Well, wait right there. There's no need to be ***that*** creative just yet. I just mean you need to embrace the mindset where you never back out of a commitment no matter how overwhelming it looks. In addition, you need to be willing to jump with both feet into a particularly scary situation when the need arises.

What Is an Entrepreneur Made of?

Here's a fact: any sound economy depends on its entrepreneurs as its strength of character. In the United States alone, it has been reported that 62% of billionaires living there are self-made, which means they, too, started from scratch like you and me. Do you want to be one of the 582 million (give or take) entrepreneurs all over the world? I bet you do. You wouldn't want to be a statistic. Neither will you want to add to the 22.5% of startup entrepreneurs who fail within their first year (Vojinovic, 2019). Given that, you need to understand just what an entrepreneur is made of.

As an entrepreneur, you need to be properly motivated to create a business from scratch. You must also be resolutely determined to complement that motivation with perseverance, self-belief, and swift decision-making. Why are these important? Keep in mind that entrepreneurship is volatile. There is bound to be an onslaught of challenges, unforeseen occurrences, and unpredictable changes that can affect you and the organization you are trying to build. Unless you are willing to make sacrifices here and there, don't expect your business to take off the ground.

You have probably heard of people who don't even have college degrees yet were able to launch successful businesses. A classic example is Richard Branson, the man behind the Virgin Group of companies – Virgin Atlantic Airways, Virgin Mobile, Virgin Records, and Virgin Galactic. Although he has a real-time net worth of $4 billion, he dropped out of high school at the age of 16 because dyslexia made it impossible for him to perform well in school

(Entreprenoria, 2016). Do you wonder how he was able to make it, eventually landing a spot in the top 500 billionaires in Forbes' list?

Branson fought through everything with sheer determination backed up by creativity and innovation. The title of this book emphasizes just how important being innovative and creative is when it comes to starting a business. A packed resume or a long list of school accomplishments is not the basis of business acumen. Just because you don't have a college degree doesn't mean you cannot make it big in the world of business. A college degree, countless medals, and overflowing achievements are just trappings meant to put you in a box. Be brave enough to get out of that box and assert your self-confidence and self-reliance.

That's because when it comes to starting a business, you don't have anything else to cling to but your own intrinsic value. That and the things you will learn in this book are what you can use to start a business using an innovative methodology. You don't even have to be a certain age in order to start a business.

Achieving Success as a Young Business Entrepreneur

Age is just a number. That's a statement that many of today's young business entrepreneurs seem to be telling us because of their tremendous success. Take it from Mark Zuckerberg, founder of Facebook, who launched the social network in his dormitory room during his college days. In fact, Zuckerberg admitted that when he started the site when he was 19, he didn't have a clear idea about the business.

Obviously, he eventually figured out how to run a company along the way and he is now considered as one of the wealthiest individuals of our time. Of course, there are some lesson we can all learn from Zuckerberg and other successful young business entrepreneurs.

- **Knowledge**

Naturally, knowledge comes first when we talk about the formula of success. Thankfully, you don't have to be an expert in your chosen field before you can begin with your business. There are countless sources for anyone eager to boost their knowledge.

Attending trainings and short courses can be an option. Other than that, reading books and browsing the internet can be valuable. Knowledge is literally at your fingertips so grab every chance to learn if you hope to hit it big.

- **Tools**

The tools you will need are highly dependent on the specific industry you aim to penetrate. For instance, getting the right machines and supplies is necessary if you are establishing a bakeshop. The same can be said regardless of what business you want to pursue.

Think of your equipment as an investment because that's what they really are. However, it's always wise to ask around before spending money. Consulting with experienced entrepreneurs can work for your advantage since it will help you avoid the same mistakes that they've done in the past.

Another tip is to keep your eyes peeled for the latest technology. Staying ahead of your competition is often necessary if you want to stand out in the crowd. As always, do some research first and honestly evaluate if some advanced tools are really needed and if you can afford them.

- **Determination**

Whether you like it or not, discouragement is part of the game - and the only way to win is to stay determined. Many young business entrepreneurs of our day can attest to that. You can't expect to be the exemption!

Hard work and discipline are key elements you need to implement perhaps especially during trying times. There are risks to take and sacrifices to be made in every step. Having the right attitude is one of the secrets effective entrepreneurs use, so don't lose focus and stay on your track.

"One of the secrets," you're probably wondering. "So there's more?" Well, these are not secret-secrets actually, if there's such a thing. I am pretty sure lots of entrepreneurs have stumbled upon these secrets time and again. The fact that I will be sharing some of the secrets I applied to my business is proof that these are not tightly-guarded secrets. These are free to anyone who wants to take them. And since we are on the subject of entrepreneurship, let me go all out and share these not-so-secret secrets to you.

Secrets of a Successful Business Entrepreneur

Establishing a business may be simple but we do not doubt that every entrepreneur can say that achieving success is entirely another matter. Of course, not all businesses hit their target and some eventually encounter failure even after just a few months in the industry. Is there any magic formula that assures victory in the endeavor?

Successful business entrepreneurs will probably tell you that there are no secret tricks – just essential ethics that need to be observed at all times. Read on as I share with you a few trade "secrets" that will lead your enterprise to greater heights.

- **Dream Big**

It may sound every cliché but dreaming big is an essential step towards success. One quotation perfectly sums it up by saying "To be without dreams is to be without hope and to be without hope is to be without purpose."

The exact same mindset applies when it comes to the business world. Having clear goals and working on achieving them one at a time is a worthwhile pursuit for every business owner.

Best-selling author Stephen Covey (The 7 Habits of Highly Effective People) describes the process as beginning "with an end in mind." Visualizing what you want your business to be in five years, for instance, makes the entire struggle worthwhile.

- **Consider Your Strengths**

Focusing on your strong points is always more effective than dwelling on your faults. Although handling a business can help you overcome several weaknesses along the way, you need to be passionate in what you do and that's where your strength will play a crucial role.

If you're a good marketer, then use that to your advantage to be a successful business entrepreneur. On the other hand, there's nothing wrong with hiring people if you're not too inclined when it comes to accounting tasks or maintaining a website.

- **Plan, Plan, Plan**

Having a plan gives you direction and writing them down gives you the chance to review them constantly. That way, you will be able to tell whether you are progressing or not. Adjustments may be needed as you proceed, so make it a point to set some time for planning.

Keep in mind that failing to plan is the same thing as planning to fail. That's something you'd want to avoid if you're serious about becoming a successful business entrepreneur.

• **Be Willing to Work Hard**

A common misconception among those dreaming about having a business is that it's easy and they don't have to work hard anymore. This is a wrong notion you may want to avoid. You'll be surprised at how hard you will need to work as a business owner. A frequent experience among start-up entrepreneurs is to work even beyond their regular schedule. If you apply all the pointers we've mentioned here, then we're sure things will be a lot easier in no time.

Since we've got that down pat already, it's time to transition into the meat of this book, which is the innovative methodology I have been babbling about from the get-go. However, before we get to that, let us first try to understand what entrepreneurial management is and why it matters when it comes to applying the aforementioned methodology.

Understanding Entrepreneurial Management

The thrust of building a business is building an institution, an organization of sorts. It's impossible to start something of a certain magnitude without considering how you'll be managing it. This is the part of starting a business that many entrepreneurs find confusing. To them, using the words entrepreneurship and management in a single context is directly oppositional. Why is that?

Think of it this way: you build a business because you want to make it on your own. The idea of working for someone else, having a manager hovering behind you, no longer appeals to you. So why in the world should you implement management practices in your business, right? Such can only stunt the business' growth. Moreover, if you have a few employees helping you run the business, you fear that implementing management practices will only encourage bureaucracy and suffocate their creativity, as well as yours.

That may be possible if we're talking about general management. The thing is, we're not. General management will not cut it as far as entrepreneurship is concerned. As I have learned in my journey as an entrepreneur, a special kind of managerial discipline is necessary when it comes to entrepreneurship. This type of management will allow entrepreneurs like you and me to harness each and every opportunity thrown our way. It is known as entrepreneurial management.

It is typically a fusion of entrepreneurial knowledge and management practices. On one hand, entrepreneurial knowledge is that which determines the skills, concepts, and mindset that a person desiring to start a business employs in an effort to grow the business. On the other hand, implementation of management practices aims to address vital management issues that a business entrepreneur faces (Price, 2011). These management issues basically relate to the following:

- A business' mission and values statement that explains what the startup is about

- Its goals and objectives, which determine the direction to which the business should go

- The business' growth strategy, which shows how the business will get to its "destination"

- The people and resources working together for the business to help it get to its destination

- An entrepreneur's organizational capabilities that establishes what structure is necessary to build and run the business

- The business' financing strategy, which decides how much money the business needs and when it is needed

- Its vision of success, which is extremely important if an entrepreneur desires to recognize his business' destination immediately

Obviously, building a business is so much easier if the right kind of management practices is enforced. In the next chapter, we will see how entrepreneurial management fares when the innovative methodology mentioned previously comes to the fore.

Key Takeaways from Chapter 1

- An entrepreneur is someone who sets up a business and takes responsibility for it.

- An entrepreneur is a risk-taker who trusts his gut feelings and is brave enough to tread on dangerous grounds.

- An entrepreneur is not compulsive. Instead, he believes in hard work.

- Entrepreneurs are any sound economy's strength of character.

- Proper motivation is necessary to build a business from the ground up.

- Not all successful entrepreneurs earned college degrees.

- An entrepreneur needs to be innovative and creative to break out of a mold and start a business.

- When it comes to business, an entrepreneur has his intrinsic value to rely on.

- Age doesn't matter when it comes to starting a business.

- There are not-so-secret secrets to becoming a successful entrepreneur.

- You can't build a startup without implementing management practices.

The right kind of management practice for startups and businesses is entrepreneurial management, which fuses entrepreneurial knowledge and management practices together.

Section 2: Innovate

In the previous section, I have already gone through the nitty-gritty of entrepreneurship. I have also mentioned several times about an innovative methodology that aims to make the most of entrepreneurial management.

In the section, "Innovate", I will try to introduce a particular methodology in the hopes of making important changes to a new business. I will also briefly discuss the difference between a startup and a business (small, medium, big, whichever floats your boat), as well as why implementing the said methodology is crucial. I don't want to preempt the proceeding chapters, but I feel it somewhat of a disservice if I don't put a label to said methodology.

So I am going out on a limb here to tell you that next few chapters you'll read will focus on the LEAN STARTUP METHODOLOGY. I will try to discuss it in detail, making sure all bases are covered so you will not have a hard time implementing it in your startup.

Chapter 2: Getting to Know the Lean Startup Methodology

Theodore Roosevelt, the twenty-sixth president of the United States who served from 1901 to 1909, once said, "Nothing worth having comes easy." That can't be truer when it comes to building a startup, and I can attest to that.

During the planning stages of my business, I was focused on how fast it can make profit and bring a return on investment and how much "richer" my bank account will be. I prematurely gauged the success of my business by how much money it will rake in for me. I failed to realize that there will be potholes and bumps along the way, and mind you, there were plenty of them.

Only after one scalding mistake after another did I understand that you can't look through rose-colored glasses when starting a business. You have to be strong enough to take whatever comes with it – pain, failures, and disappointments included. It was foolish of me to think I can relish the positives and avoid the negatives altogether. It was only after I sat down and started analyzing things did I realize that before ultimately reaching success, I will need to weather the storm first.

And weather the storm I did, but not after taking the time to fully and truly understand that I needed something to guide me, see me through the entire journey. That something turned out to be the lean startup methodology, which, for all intents and purposes, can be considered the brainchild of Eric Ries, entrepreneur, blogger, and author of the book "The Lean Startup: How Today's Entrepreneurs Use Continuous Innovation to Create Radically Successful Businesses".

In the book, Ries gamely shares that this innovative method traces its roots to the lean manufacturing revolution that was developed by two Japanese men working for Toyota (Ries, 2011, p. 28). I will not go into the nitty-gritty of the book, but I will try to explain the lean startup methodology as best as I can based on how I understand it. I am quite confident I can explain it; after all, I have applied it in my business and have seen how beneficial it is.

Unmasking Lean Startup Methodology

At this point, you're probably looking at the lean startup method in the same way you will a recipe – a list of ingredients right there, step-by-step procedures right here, and finally, the finished dish. However, recipes can be tweaked to suit your palate. You can tone down the taste of a dish or make it even more savory depending on your mood. That isn't the case with the lean startup. There are no tweaks to this method. If you do it right, then this methodology will definitely be the perfect model to use for building a startup.

Lean startup is a system specifically introduced by Ries to entrepreneurs who have expressed their desire to create businesses. And just to be clear, a startup is different from a [small, medium, or big] business. Yes, that is a point of confusion among entrepreneurs; they think the two are one and the same. It's important that you know the differences between the two since such knowledge can influence your decision when it comes to actually starting your business.

One of the starkest differences between a startup and a small business (we're here using the term small business loosely) is that the former is meant to be ***temporary*** while the latter, depending on how foolproof your business plan, is virtually ***evergreen***. Another difference is the motivating force behind the business – a startup is founded with the intent to disturb the market with a business model that's scalable and has an impact on the market while a small business is founded by someone who wants to be the boss of himself, someone who wants to secure an established presence among his competition (Pope, 2019).

Funding source for a startup and a small business differs, too. Initially, both may be funded by the entrepreneur's own money or a loan from a financial institution. Nevertheless, once a startup takes off the ground and becomes successful, further funding is secured typically from a venture capitalist. Moreover, because a startup is usually identified with tech companies, it's a tad riskier to create than a small business.

That is not to say, though, that small businesses are better than startups. In fact, there are common pitfalls associated with small businesses, specifically as regards marketing strategies, as you will read next.

The Common Pitfalls of Small Business Marketing

Marketing is considered by many as one of the most important investments for any small business. Without it, your target customers may never know about you, your products or services offered, or why buying from you is a better decision than buying from your competition. As a result, your products or services go unnoticed.

Marketing is a broad discipline and entrepreneurs must be able to overcome the pitfalls of small business marketing in order for your business to succeed.

Consider this a bonus section that will outline and discuss some of the most common pitfalls of small business marketing. This particular section will defnitely provide you with useful insights that can help improve your marketing strategies and methods. That way, whether you're starting a small business or you're more likely to brave your way into a startup, you will know what you shoud and shouldn't do if you want a successful business that follows the lean startup methodology.

1. Defining Target Markets

Who do you plan to target? Where can you find them? This thing may seem like a very basic matter, but the groundwork of your marketing efforts actually starts here. If you want to achieve marketing success, you need to have a clear concept of who your target market will be. Create a brief narrative or profile of your target customer. Jot it down and polish it; collaborate with your team; figure out what your target client uses as its buying criteria. Defining who your ideal customer is will help you put everything in order and customize your marketing efforts based on their needs and wants.

2. Creating a Marketing Plan

Every small-scale entrepreneur must have a marketing plan to support their business goals. If developing a marketing plan is a challenge, there are plenty of resources on the Internet that can provide you with marketing plan templates. To give you an idea of what you should include in your plan, download some of these templates and use them as a guide. Be sure to keep it short and limit it to three pages if you can. If you can afford it, get a marketing specialist who can help you develop the plan.

3. Finding Resources for Marketing

One of the most common pitfalls of small business marketing is the cost of advertising, but small businesses cannot afford not to invest the time and money into this thing. Buying a full-page Saturday newspaper ad or NBA TV commercials is usually not a financial dilemma for large-scale businesses. However, such costs are obviously a predicament for many small businesses. To overcome this, spend some time studying and exploring what you can achieve with the low-cost marketing methods that are now available to small businesses.

4. Getting Referrals

Most small business entrepreneurs will probably agree that referrals are an important asset to their business. Even so, many remain cautious when openly asking for referrals. If you want to grow your business, be sure to let your existing customers, as well as your network of contacts, come to the realization that their referrals are a great help to your business. Try to make referrals an integral part of your marketing strategies so you can expand your reach and widen your customer base.

5. Increasing Sales Conversions

If you are faced with this common pitfall of small business marketing, try to look again at your marketing message. Deal with this challenge by making sure that you make a relevant and attractive offer to your intended customers. Before running a marketing campaign, test it first and then refine it. Small businesses cannot afford to only invest on advertisements that build image or brand. You can develop and promote your company image while causing increased sales by providing an offer to motivate your target customers to take action within a specific period of time. In general, your promotional campaign should focus on eliciting a response from your target customers that translates into sales while building your brand at the same time.

Whatever industry you are in, it is very likely that you would encounter one or more of the common pitfalls of small business marketing. Fortunately, there are ways to overcome this dilemma. All you have to do is explore your options and be creative in your marketing methods.

Now that you know the difference between the two, as well as the common pitfalls associated with marketing a small business, let's go back to the discussion on hand – the lean startup methodology. As the name of this innovative method implies, it was founded with startup entrepreneurs at the forefront of Ries' mind. Why do I say so?

We've mentioned earlier that a startup is riskier to create than a small business. Risk is the epitome of a startup because you are practically venturing into the unknown. Some of you have probably done it. I have done it. I have left a stable job just so I can start my own business without even considering what will become of me in case things don't go according to plan.

The risk factor of startup businesses is what prompted the idea of the lean startup. Its founder wanted to lend companies of all sizes a hand, so to speak, to help them navigate through rough waters and lower the risk factors through three things – minimum viable products or MVPs, painstaking experimentation, and full commitment to learning (McGowan, 2017). In a nutshell, the lean startup methodology centers on the creation of a sustainable business where minimal time and money is wasted.

Think of it this way: you spend an obscene amount of money trying to come up with products that you think the consuming public will love, "*you think*" being the operative words. Did you even stop to think if the products you're creating can solve a particular problem or address a pressing situation? You probably didn't, and guess what? You're more than likely to fail. Scratch that. YOU WILL FAIL.

Harsh words, right? However, I'm speaking the truth, and that is something that Ries' realized as well.

Earlier, I said that Ries' concept of the lean startup method was developed because of two Japanese men who worked for Toyota – Taiichi Ohno and Shigeo Shingo. Observing how these two worked, Ries' saw how the entire process of building Japanese cars worked – waste is reduced and eliminated, if at all, in order to release the cars at the lowest cost and without sacrificing the high value of the cars. Through his observation, Ries' was able to visualize a system that can likewise be applied by entrepreneurs.

Understanding the Lean Startup Methodology

If you read through the introduction of Section 1 of this book (and I am sure you did), then you probably remembered my mentioning that a bit of science is necessary to guarantee a sustainable business. That scientific element is actually the lean startup methodology, which can be construed as a scientific approach as far as creating and managing a business goes. At the cusp of it is ensuring that customers get the products or services they paid for in no time.

For all intents and purposes, the lean startup methodology is like a diagram that teaches entrepreneurs how to navigate through a new business – how to steer it to the right direction, when to turn, and when to keep up with the current pace to reach the destination. More than that, however, this innovative methodology aims to teach entrepreneurs how they can grow a business by going "full steam ahead". The lean startup particularly works for businesses where product development is a major catalyst to sustaining the business.

Remember how in the previous subheading I mentioned that some new entrepreneurs fail in product development because they create products that they think people want? They don't take into consideration the actual needs and wants of consumers, so they spend copious amount of time, energy, and money to "perfect" products without giving consumers a chance to give their two cents.

Finally, when the products bomb, they immediately blame other factors – poor marketing, wrong concept, et cetera, et cetera. What they failed to realize is they never asked potential consumers if the products they're conceptualizing are interesting. I am not saying each manufactured product should be given the green light by consumers. I am basically explaining that when it comes to product development, the voice of consumers matter *a lot*, and unfortunately, that's something many entrepreneurs overlook.

Nevertheless, through the implementation of the lean startup methodology, entrepreneurs who are in the planning stages of product development are persuaded to raise questions along the way – from the time the initial ideas are set forth up to the point where design choices are made, or additional features are given consideration.

Such questioning is considered an important process of the lean startup methodology since it allows entrepreneurs to potentially come up with their MVPs. In turn, the MVPs need to be shown to a few chosen test customers who will then decide if the products need further improvements or whatnot. Do you see how beneficial such testing is?

An Alternative to the Business Plan

You can think of the lean startup methodology as an alternative to a business plan. If you are not convinced that your plan is sound, you have the option to run a business based on the lean startup approach. It can work like a prototype that can test if your concepts or strategies can work in an actual business. A lean or small operation can still cost you some investment, but it will not cost you much in case your strategies do not work. Yet, with a lean operation, the business stands a good chance of surviving.

If successful and as this prototype grows, you will still need a good plan to support your bigger operation in order to know how much more funds you will need to accommodate growth, to help you compete better, and to stay focused on your set goals.

Whether you opt for a plan or a prototype, remember that for your business to survive and succeed you need to know what will make your business tick, which ones will be your competitors, what your common products are going to be, and what benefits you can offer your customers. Being unique is important. After sales, customer service seals relationships. Understanding competition can give you the edge in the market.

The Build-Measure-Learn Concept

As an entrepreneur, the abovementioned process will prevent you from manufacturing thousands of products, which are not foolproof, from the get-go. Instead, you'll only be manufacturing a few products for the test customers; thus, you save time and money from production. You may not see the difference it makes immediately, but the feedback you'll get from the first set of test customers will help you see what works, what doesn't, and where to go from there. Only when the products are proven highly marketable will actual production take place. It's a win-win.

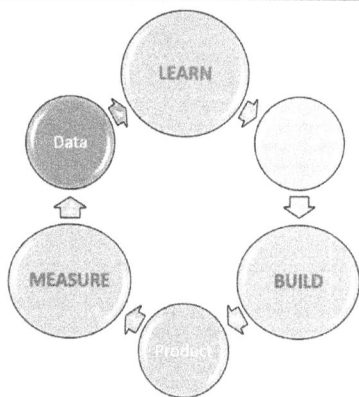

Build – Measure – Learn Feedback Loop

LEARN

Data

MEASURE

BUILD

Product

And that, ladies and gentlemen, is the crux of the lean startup methodology. It is hinged on the "build, measure, learn" model that Ries came up with, and that model is meant to be followed repeatedly until such time that the MVPs become actual offerings that can sustain a business. More importantly, the repeated cycle of that build-measure-learn model leads to innovation, which is the main thrust of the second section of this book.

It All Winds down to Innovation

How does innovation fit into all these? Just think. By adhering to the build-measure-learn model, the feedback you get from test customers will allow you to turn from one product idea or niche to another in the hopes of coming up with an even better product. It is risky, yes, but that's the whole concept of a startup; it's all about the risks you need to take. Otherwise, you'll never know what works and what doesn't.

Believe me when I say to innovate my business was the furthest thing from my mind back then. I figured, "Why should I meddle with something that is already working?" However, after applying the lean startup methodology, I realized there are still areas in which I can significantly improve the quality and reliability of what I offer consumers.

Indeed, even if I already had a structured idea, there was no harm in tapping into my creativity in order to come up with better ways to test my products. What worked can stay put, but I deduced that I can always come up with a new and improved version that my loyal customer base will certainly take notice of. In addition, even if I had minimal resources, I was able to innovate.

Here is a classic example of how the build-measure-learn model can be applied to a business. Let's say you're a fitness enthusiast and have decided to launch a healthy meal prep delivery service. Initially, your goal is to target busy, single people in their 20s in urban areas.

You figured these 20-somethings are always on the go and are busy making their mark as yuppies and food prep may be furthest from their minds.

However, since there is no hard and fast rule regarding who can and cannot order from your delivery service, even those outside your target age group have started ordering, too. In fact, your healthy meal preps have a **better market** among 30-something new moms who live in affluent suburbs. Will you stick to your original target market? Perhaps. Nevertheless, you can always add more delivery schedules, as well as types of healthy foods to prepare that addresses the nutritional needs of new moms who may be nursing. Eventually, you may start prepping healthy meals for these new moms' husbands and other children.

Obviously, you didn't stick to a one-track game plan. You changed its course based on what the needs of the consuming public were. That is how lean startup's build-measure-learn model works.

That's the central concept of the lean startup method. That is not to say, though, that things get easier from there. When I took on the build-measure-learn model, I honestly thought I had it down pat. Boy was I wrong! It took me a while to realize that it was a research-intensive process. In fact, I had to tap into the humble storehouse of knowledge I built while I was still in school to recall the six parts of the scientific method!

See what I did there? I have been saying that the lean startup methodology is scientific in its own right, and I will tell you why. I'm sure you still remember those six key elements that characterize the scientific method:

- Questions

- Hypotheses

- Experiments

- Observations

- Analyses

- Conclusions

Relating the abovementioned to the lean startup method, I mentioned previously that questioning (questions) is an important process of lean startup since it paves the way for entrepreneurs to come up with their MVPs (hypothesis). Then, once the products are ready, these are sent out to test customers (experiment). The test customers' feedback (observation) will help entrepreneurs tweak the products (analysis). Once the products have been improved, these are deemed marketable (conclusion).

It is an on-going cycle, one that can weigh you down emotionally especially when feedback from test customers comes in. Imagine the sheer agony of putting your products out there before these are even deemed marketable and embracing whatever feedback the test customers give. They can give you sugar-coated feedback, or they can blatantly brutal; it doesn't matter. You need to be tough enough to take in everything they have to say about the products and find the strength to implement it.

So, yes, the lean startup methodology isn't all sunshine and rainbows. Nevertheless, if you apply it well and do it properly, it can help you create a business that actually, sincerely caters to the needs of its consumer base. And when customers are satisfied, you can expect repeat business. Hence, you are able to grow and sustain your business, which is the idea behind your entrepreneurship.

Key Takeaways from Chapter 2

- Starting a business isn't all sunshine and rainbows. There is bound to be mishaps, and you need to be prepared for those.

- The lean startup methodology can't be tweaked. You need to follow through on that model to build a business.

- The lean startup method is perfect for startup entrepreneurs who live and breathe risks.

- Simply put, the lean startup methodology focuses on creating a sustainable business that wastes very little time and money.

- The lean startup method is built around the build-measure-learn concept.

- Adhering to the build-measure-learn concept allows for innovation of products and services.

- The six key elements of the scientific method can be applied when you follow the lean startup methodology.

- Innovation makes for a sustainable business.

We have skimmed the surface of the lean startup methodology in this chapter. In the next one, I will explain the five principles upon which this innovative methodology is anchored. Hopefully, at the end of the chapter, I will have shared with you several takeaways that can prove to be gold nuggets of helpful learnings as you build your business.

Chapter 3: Five Principles behind the Lean Startup Methodology

Believe it or not, the lean startup methodology has had its fair share of criticisms, both constructive and destructive. For instance, some people said it's already an easy enough process; thus, oversimplifying it seemed redundant. So many blogs have been written about the subject claiming the lean startup is already simple – all of its basic elements are there to explore – so why make it simpler?

Well, dissatisfaction is, perhaps, human nature. It's impossible to please everybody. Here's the thing, though: inasmuch as the lean startup may seem simple, it's one heck of a complex system. ***You think you know*** what to do with it, but once you're actually doing it, you'll realize its intricacy.

Moreover, just as it is with any other system, you can't just window-shop for the parts you "like", choose those, and leave the rest behind. No. It's impossible to make a system work without tapping on all its parts to work seamlessly together. And that's what makes the lean startup multifaceted.

Like I have said earlier, it's a research-intensive process. You can't downplay the importance of research since it will gauge whether or not you're up for the challenge. If, during the course of research, you realize you're not cut out for the lean startup method, you're free to consider a different approach. At least, you haven't expended much time, effort, energy, and money yet since you're still on the research phase. On the other hand, if you think you can take on the challenge, by all means, go!

Perhaps understanding the five principles on which the lean startup is hinged will help you see if it's something you can work with. That's what I did, and that's why I can freely talk about the methodology in this book. I'm not saying

I'm an expert at this method, but I try to apply what I learn (after all, it's a continuous process). And that's what I want you to do, too.

The Lean Startup Principles

Principle is defined as a fundamental truth serving as the cornerstone of a particular system of belief or reasoning. With that said, it's only right to assume that the lean startup methodology is founded on a set of fundamental truths that govern how it works. In this part of the book, I will try to expound on those five principles that are behind the lean startup methodology (The Lean Startup, n.d.).

1. ***Entrepreneurs are everywhere.*** Unlike regular employees who are cooped up in their offices from nine to five, entrepreneurs (self-made people, if you will) are found just about everywhere. You can create a startup from your garage or your bedroom (or dorm room like Mark Zuckerberg). That's

the beauty of entrepreneurship: it, in itself, is a human institution from which innovative products and services can be created regardless if conditions are uncertain. With entrepreneurs being everywhere, it goes without saying that the lean startup method will work anywhere, regardless of the size of a business or which sector of the industry it belongs to.

2. ***Entrepreneurship is management.*** Just because it's a self-made business doesn't mean management practices can't be applied. Like I have discussed in the early goings of this book, there is such a thing as entrepreneurial management. It's a type of management specifically geared towards entrepreneurship. Keep in mind that entrepreneurship is a human institution, not a product or service, and an institution cannot function fully unless capable hands are managing it.

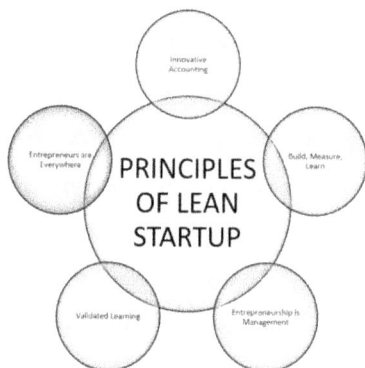

PRINCIPLES OF LEAN STARTUP

- Innovative Accounting
- Build, Measure, Learn
- Entrepreneurship is Management
- Validated Learning
- Entrepreneurs are Everywhere

3. **Validated learning.** You don't create a business with the sole purpose of making money or being at your customers' beck and call. Heck, you don't even create it, so you'll have an excuse to make products or formulate services. You start a business with the aim of learning how to make it sustainable. Remember how I said the six parts of the scientific method applies to the lean startup method? Well, the experiment part applies when you need to validate your learnings

scientifically to see whether these work. It's a continuous process.

4. ***Build-Measure-Learn.*** Ah, if it isn't our favorite concept. Seriously, though, this three-step concept is basically what makes the lean startup methodology tick. Overall, the primary activity of a startup business, as you can see in the illustration in Chapter 2, is to formulate ideas, turn these ideas into viable products (build), see how customers react to the products (measure), and use customers' feedbacl to see whether you need to go to a new direction or continue until the product becomes marketable (learn). It's an on-going loop intended to accelerate the growth of a business.

5. ***Innovation accounting.*** In the lean startup method, it's important to measure certain metrics like how much progress you're making, how milestones should be set up, and which task should be prioritized. Implementing

entrepreneurial management whole making sure these metrics are met can be difficult. Hence, innovation accounting is necessary. This novel type of accounting is specifically designed for startup businesses. Its use is the only way you can figure out if you are, indeed, making progress or if your efforts are for naught. This particular principle of the lean startup focuses on numbers that are pivotal for the growth of your business like engagement and customer acquisition cost.

Are you now fully convinced that you should try the lean startup methodology for your business? If you're still having second thoughts, then perhaps this next segment will tickle your fancy even more.

Is Adapting the Lean Startup Methodology Necessary?

I have been giving you the 411 about the lean startup methodology almost from the get-go, but I am quite sure you're still adamant about giving it a try. After all, it's the fate of your business at stake here. One wrong move and everything you have worked and been working hard for can go down the drain.

Of course, I can always convince you that *it did work* for me. However, what works for one will not always work for another, right? That's why I still want to share some reasons why I think you should adapt the lean startup in your business. In fact, these reasons will work whether yours is a new business or already an established organization.

1. Regardless if you're a startup or an existing business, you are bound to create new products or services. Hence, you will potentially be reaching new markets. Adapting the lean startup methodology will help your business

decrease cycle time, gather customer feedback faster, and reduce waste.

2. There will be new processes you will want to employ in your business, processes that will certainly have a bearing on your customer base. So you want to ensure the best results by deploying a customer-validated process. Through the lean startup, you will get continuous feedback and validation.

3. You may already have a five-year projection in place. In a volatile environment, that five-year plan may not succeed. Nevertheless, adapting the lean startup will bring in the agility and speed you need so you can adapt in an ever-changing environment. It will certainly help you go a long way.

4. Adapting the lean startup methodology will help you foster innovation in your business minus the wasted money.

5. With the lean startup backing you up every step of the way, you will not be

overly concerned about the success and adaption rates of the new digitized system you are planning to deploy.

Keep in mind that two of the main purposes of this methodology are: to make your business competitive in such a cutthroat environment and drive growth. In a nutshell, here are some benefits of adapting the method:

- Throughout the course of adapting the process, you stay focused on your goals and you get clear **visibility** of which direction you plan on going.

- The process gives you a heads up when it's time to make necessary changes to the strategies you are currently using. As a result, you spend **less time, effort, and money**.

- By the time your product or service is deemed marketable, you will have already **established a customer base**. This includes the test customers you reached out to during the build-measure-learn phase.

- The process/es you will create using the lean startup will already have been ***tried and tested***.

The lean startup method is focused on five key points:

- Speed

- Flexibility

- Innovation

- Customer focus

- Elimination of uncertainties

Key Takeaways from Chapter 3

- The lean startup methodology may seem simple, but it's an intricate web of complexities that you need to carefully study.

- It's a multifaceted process that is research-intensive.

- There are five principles, fundamental truths, which govern the implementation of the lean startup method.

- There are at least five reasons why it is imperative to adapt the lean startup methodology in any business (whether startup or already established).

- There are four key benefits to adapting the lean startup.

- The lean startup method if focused on five key points – speed, flexibility, innovation, customer satisfaction, and eliminate uncertainties.

This section of the book really laid bare the ins and outs of the lean startup methodology. So far, I have provided you insight on how to create a business using the build-measure-learn model. I have also helped you see how the lean startup can help make innovations to your business.

At this point, we are heading on to the third section of the book, which will discuss how the lean startup methodology figures inasmuch as the acceleration of your business is concerned.

Section 3: Accelerate

To accelerate literally means to gain speed. In the just-concluded chapter, I made mention of the fact that one of the reasons why the lean startup method works for most businesses is it allows for speed, especially when it comes to dealing with unwarranted circumstances.

In the third section, "Accelerate", we will see how adapting the lean startup method can boost the speed in which a business grows. Along the way, we will also discuss how acceleration, as it relates to this awesome methodology, factors in with other aspects of a business.

Chapter 4: Grow Your Business with Maximum Acceleration

Are you guys still with me? I really hope so, because I am positive the learnings you'll get from this book will be extremely beneficial for your business. We have been going back and forth about the subject of lean startup methodology (as is to be expected since it is what the book's all about). And so far, we have pooled together three key takeaways about lean startup – it teaches you how to drive a startup, it teaches you when you need to pivot or turn to another direction, and it teaches you when to continue going.

These key takeaways have a common goal in mind – to help you, the entrepreneur, to grow your business with maximum acceleration. And as we have been discussing from the get-go, the main thrust of the lean startup method is for entrepreneurs like you and me to embrace a principled approach when it comes to product development. Why do you think so?

Well, history will show that there are far too many failed startups and a trail of broken hearts after it. These startups failed because while they spent a considerable amount of time perfecting what they think is an awesome product, they didn't take one important factor into consideration – customers' feedback. In their excitement to build a product they think will rake in thousands in revenue, they disregarded the feelings of customers, so to speak, and never bothered asking them if the product was interesting or not.

Only when the customers state voicing their dissatisfaction, their indifference towards the product, will entrepreneurs realize they made a mistake. However, it may be too late already.

The lean startup methodology aims to eliminate that one-track mindset of entrepreneurs. I will boldly tell you that if you want to succeed, stop thinking about yourself and start thinking about your prospective customers. If you start putting the interests of your customers ahead of anything else, you will accelerate the growth of your business in no time.

The last thing you want is to have uncertainties when running your business. The lean startup approach helps you eliminate such. How? By building or creating a product that you will let test customers sample and by absorbing the feedbacks you'll get from these customers, you will avoid second-guessing. With a prototype, you will not be wasting as much money as you will if you marketed a product that people will not buy. With a prototype, you'll get to find out what works, what doesn't, and what changes or tweaks you need to make.

By applying these changes, you will come up with a product that is not only marketable but also one that already has an established customer base. That's because the same test customers will more than likely buy the product knowing that their two cents were taken into consideration during product development.

Acceleration Is Easy-Peasy

If there is one universal truth that's common in some business owners, it is that over time, lethargy creeps in and gets the better of them. When that happens, everyone, from the business owner to his smallest employee loses the enthusiasm that has been the driving force from the get-go. Once this enthusiasm is lost, everything is bound to start crumbling down, which can lead to the demise of the business.

If it isn't lethargy that will lead to the untimely death of a business, then, it most likely will be bureaucracy. That means the business owner will strictly and precisely define rules and procedures that each and every one in the company needs to follow to a T. Such type of authority can stunt the growth of a business since no one else except the business owner has the freedom to explore things that can lead to the improvement of the business.

As a startup business owner, you will want to avoid lethargy and bureaucracy at all cost. Yes, both are not the end-all and be-all of a business.

With the right driving force, you can make your business succeed and never lose the agility or speed it had from the start. In fact, if you apply the lean startup approach to your business, you will be able to sustain and maintain its agility and speed, not to mention its disposition to learning new approaches and methodologies. Most importantly, you will find it easier to cultivate a work environment that embraces unorthodox thinking; thus, there is more room for growth and innovation.

And for a business that dreams of scaling in the fastest amount of time possible, applying the lean startup method can serve to accelerate the business. How? Well, the lean startup approach encourages the practice of doing things in small batches. Ries explains this in his book in which he used the example of Japanese carmaker Toyota and its car production technique post-World War II. Apparently, American carmakers were then mass-producing their automobiles using extremely huge batch sizes that demanded huge amounts of money. These Americans figured mass-producing the cars will bring down the cost of each part and make the cars inexpensive. Moreover, the cars will be totally uniform.

However, since the car market for the Japanese was way smaller, they had to take on a different approach to their car production. Ohno and Shingo, mentioned in an earlier chapter, innovated Toyota's car-making methodology by using general-purpose machines that were much smaller and able to produce small batches of different parts in one go. These two Japanese reconfigured each machine to meet the "by batch" demand. As a result, Toyota manufactured cars in small batches.

Do you think the smaller batch approach slowed down the car-production of Toyota? On the contrary, Toyota was able to produce different product varieties at a much faster pace. The company was able to address the smaller demands of its fragmented market while keeping in step with its mass-producing competition. Toyota kept to this system of production while increasing the size of its market, and by 2008, it became the largest carmaker **in the world** (Ries, 2011, p. 182).

Now you're probably thinking, "What does Toyota's example have to do with my business? Mine is dramatically smaller." That may be true. However, if you apply the same system to your business, you will be leaving a smaller room for second-guessing. Envision this scenario: you produce a product in big batches only to realize only a couple of your customers actually want it. Think of the time, energy, and money you will have wasted trying to build the product that only two people loved. If you produced in small batches, though, even if only two people supported the product, you will not have wasted as much time, effort, and money.

Sticking to the abovementioned system will eventually lead to sustainable growth. Here, I use the term sustainable growth specifically in the context of a startup business applying the lean startup methodology. A business using this method is practically accelerating its growth potential since the system makes accelerated production feasible. And do you know the possibilities of such?

When a business is able to produce more quality products in a short amount of time, return on investment is faster. Not only that. Keep in mind that your production is now based on the build-measure-learn model, which means customer feedback is at the forefront. From this point on, your succeeding productions will already be based on the feedback you received from test customers. Then, when the product has reached its marketable status, your test customers will be the first ones to buy it. Since the product is now made according to their "specifications", customer satisfaction is guaranteed. And when customers are satisfied, you can expect an onslaught of new customers.

Yes, your past customers' behavior affects the influx of new customers, which translates to sustainable growth. In what ways?

- When customers are satisfied with a product, they are bound to tell others about it. Containing their enthusiasm will be futile, and once they start telling their friends and family about it, the curiosity of these people will move them to try the product themselves.

- When customers use a product, awareness of the product is imminent. Everytime the product is used, other people are knowingly or unknowingly exposed to it and may be influenced to buy it.

- A business may pay its customers to advertise the product through their social media pages or blogs. Payment will usually come from revenues that sales from these customers generated. They become influencers in their own right and are more than likely to entice others to try the product out.

- A product may be designed for repeated purchases. An example of this is a grooming subscription box for men. Such product is released monthly, and since the box contains different products each month, men will buy it every month.

The abovementioned catalysts of sustainable growth are all made possible through accelerated production.

Key Takeaways from Chapter 4

- The principled approach of lean startup helps you grow your business with maximum acceleration.

- Many startups fail because they disregard the feelings of customers.

- Customer dissatisfaction often moves business owners to do some serious self-examination to see in which areas they can improve.

- The lean startup methodology will help business entrepreneurs focus on improving customer satisfaction.

- Lethargy and bureaucracy can lead to the untimely death of a startup.

- Sticking to the lean startup methodology can lead to a startup's sustainable growth.

- Past customers' behaviors can be catalysts for sustainable growth.

I have just finished sharing what I know about accelerating a business through the lean startup methodology. In the next chapter, I will be talking about the lean startup technology in action.

Chapter 5: The Lean Startup Technology in Action

We are nearing the end of this book, and I am pretty sure your curiosity has been piqued greatly about the lean startup technology, and rightfully so. After all, we have discussed many ways in which it can maximize the accelerated growth of your business. In this section, I will talk about the lean startup methodology as you observe it *in action*.

One specific area I will talk about in relation to lean startup is how you can efficiently manage your employees using the methodology (Sheth, 2019). It's a vital approach that ensures continuous progress for your business. Nevertheless, you need to anticipate that trials and errors will be part of the process since you will need to continue experimenting, testing, and investigating whatever it is your offering, whether products or services, repeatedly as these develop.

You will notice the stark difference between a business that follows the lean startup methodology and a traditional startup. A traditional startup follows a methodological process that is built on long-term vision, strategy, and plans. On the other hand, a business following the lean startup will expedite the processes by going through the steps I have discussed in the previous sections of this book. Another difference is that information about the products or services will be kept to a minimum few – employees, investors, and test customers – until such time that the offerings are deemed marketable, keeping in mind that the entire process is done in stealth mode.

By now you're probably wondering, "What do all these have to do with effective employee management?" The answer is quite simple, actually. The more streamlined process offers managers a chance to discern whether or not there are some inefficiencies with the current processes. Thus, they can correct or change whatever needs correction and only deliver to customers what they deserve – value for money.

Bonds Strengthened Because of Lean

Another example of the lean startup technology in action is the development of a strong A-team. Because the build-measure-learn process is put in effect, the right people are hired and put in the right place. As a result, each one is given tasks based on the skills they possess, as well as their adaptability to the lean startup methodology. As your business grows, you can transition your first batch of employees, you're A-team, as brand marketers. This time, their job will be to talk about your business to others. This will result in a chain reaction of sorts in which brand awareness is raised without you having to invest money. In turn, this awareness will start raking in revenue and improve the confidence of your employees.

Once their confidence level is improved, they can go ahead and train a fresh group of employees with the same vision they had when they started with you. This unified faith in the vision and mission of your business is crucial because as much as possible, you want to have people working collectively for you to help you reach your main goal.

How to Get Started with an Effective Lean Startup A-Team

Here's the thing: a business' A-team doesn't just fall automatically down from the sky. In fact, one of the key elements in forming an A-team for your business using the lean startup approach is to hire people based only on the open positions. If there are no open positions in the business, then don't hire people. That is the best way to keep the business efficient. Moreover, because the lean startup methodology is somewhat of an unorthodox approach to starting a business, another vital element to forming your A-team is to choose people who will fit ideally to the lean startup culture you are trying to cultivate.

Then, you will want to entice these employees comprising your A-team to stay with your company by offering them something tangible. Knowing what an employee can bring to the table to add a unique value to your business can help you determine what sort of "incentive" you'll offer them.

Some businesses that follow the lean startup methodology offer employee stock ownership plan (ESOP) to their employees. An ESOP is a benefit plan, an equity, in which employees are given ownership interest in a business (Ganti, 2019). The ESOP, as mentioned earlier, will be based on a distinctive skill that an employee can offer to make the business better.

Why should you, the business owner, go through such great lengths to keep your current roster of employees that comprise your business' A-team? Well, most of those employees left the security that corporate jobs offer just to join a new business. It is such a huge leap of faith, one that requires you to make them see that the big risk they took was not for nothing. They will have something to gain out of their big move. On the flipside, you need to make sure the incentives you will offer the employees will not, in any way, impede with business activities. You need to ensure the company stays protected and that every business activity is always carried out in a professional manner.

If you decide to give your employees ESOP, you need to ensure you're doing it properly. There needs to be a structure you will follow to make sure the process flows smoothly. Perhaps a good way to decide how much an employee will get is to have a pre-determined range of equity stake. This percentage will be paid over and above the salary that an employee receives. Here's a model you can follow:

- Rank-and-File Employees and Junior Managers – 0.2 to 0.33%

- Managers and Senior Lead Managers – 0.33 to 0.66%

- Directors – 0.4 to 1.25%

- Product Development Leads and Engineers – 0.5 to 1%

- Independent Board Members – 1%

- Vice Presidents – 1 to 2%

- Chief Operating Officer (COO) – 2 to 5%

- Chief Executive Officer (CEO) – 5 to 10%

As you can see, the bracket range above includes everyone, from the rank-and-file employees to the business founder(s). Keep in mind that the above is just a model you can use in your own business. There is no hard and fast rule as far as range brackets go. You will decide on the best compensation; thus, it's vital that you fully understand the types of ESOPs you can offer to employees.

A flexible schedule is yet another thing you can offer employees. Believe it or not, there are people who work best during daytime and there are those who work best after the sun has set. If that is the case with your current roster of employees, then by all means, yield to the schedule that allows them to function in their fullest potential and efficiency.

Really now, if you want to keep your top employees happy, you need to learn how to be flexible especially when it comes to their work hours. Applying the lean startup methodology in your business will allow your employees to either work together in teams following a rotational schedule or anytime that is convenient to them. If you will opt for the flexible schedule, then you may want to consider allowing some of your employees to work from home, too.

Another way to allow for flexibility in a lean startup "environment" is to veer away from setting hours for team members. Try giving project-based work that follows a specific timeline. This means there is only a set number of hours they have to get the job done.

Indeed, the lean startup methodology can do wonders to improve the efficiency of employees. Nevertheless, it will all depend on how "understanding" of their circumstances you are as an employer. If you're unyielding, then the growth of the business will be stunted no matter how hard you try to implement the lean startup approach.

The whole idea of adopting a lean startup culture in a business is to help it improve continuously. If you will not be open to changes, continuous improvements in your business, no matter if these are big or small, will be impossible. Remember, a business that applies the lean startup approach revolves around change.

Just make sure everyone of your employees, from the lowest to highest rung of the ladder, is aware when changes are implemented. It doesn't matter what the changes are about. The changes are meant to benefit not only the business as a whole but also each and every one of your employees. Hence, you need to make them aware of the changes if you want them to be on the same page as you are during the implementation period.

Every one of the people comprising a "lean startup team" must be moving in the same direction. That is the key to the successful implementation of the lean startup methodology. Employee's commitment, whether you're the CEO or a rank-and-filer, is necessary since the whole idea of the lean startup is everyone having a shared purpose to foster a culture of improvement in a business.

Key Takeaways from Chapter 5

- The lean startup approach can help you manage your employees efficiently.

- Following the lean startup methodology in a business can help managers discern if there are inefficiencies with the current processes and be able to remedy these right away.

- The bond between your business' elite employees and those in the lower rung of the ladder becomes stronger because of the lean startup approach.

- One way to get started with the lean startup application is by giving deserving employees some sort of "incentive".

- Flexibility in their work schedule is one way to improve the efficiency of employees.

- If you want to efficiently manage your employees using the lean startup approach, you need to learn how to "yield" to changes.

- A business adopting the lean startup methodology centers on continuous small improvements for the betterment of the business.

- Every one of the employees, from the highest to the lowest rank, must be on the same page for the continuous improvement of the business adopting the lean startup approach.

I have probably covered everything there is to discuss about the lean startup methodology and why using it in a business is advantageous. In the final chapter of this book, I will try to summarize everything we have come to know about the lean startup methodology to make it even easier for you to apply it in your business.

Chapter 6: Summarizing the Key Points of the Lean Startup Methodology

Applying the lean startup methodology in a business (whether it's a typical business setup or a startup) significantly changes its landscape. And the ensuing effect will depend on how yours adapt to the process. It certainly isn't a one-size-fits-all kind of thing, and that's why it's called a methodology in the first place. There is a system in place that you will need to follow, otherwise, your efforts may be for naught.

Thus far, we have discussed in detail how the lean startup methodology works. Nevertheless, with the amount of information we covered, you may be overwhelmed at this point. That is why I have decided to summarize the key points of the lean startup methodology to make it easier for you to apply it in your business.

In a nutshell, the lean startup approach is all about finding out what it is your customers want right away (or perhaps as soon as you decide to start a business). It is also about adapting to the needs of your customers through continuous testing and feedback-gathering without wasting any of your financial investments.

I divided this book into three sections CREATE, INNOVATE, and ACCELERATE.

In the first section, I endeavored to explain what entrepreneurship is all about and why entrepreneurial management matters especially in a new business. In the second section, I discussed the lean startup methodology in detail and explained why using this methodology in your business will be for its best interests. Finally, in the third section, I showed you how adapting the lean startup method can boost the growth of your business.

Key Takeaways from the Entire Book

- The lean startup methodology is all about creating or developing products or services that customers actually want.

- This innovative methodology aims to do away with wasted time, effort, and money by making sure products or services only come out for actual consumption or use once these are deemed marketable. Otherwise, the products or services will go through a special cycle.

- The leans startup methodology's groundwork is the build-measure-learn process. This means after producing something, you take the time to measure how it will fare with your target customers by going through a testing period. This testing period will let you know whether or not the products or services you offer need further enhancements or improvements.

- The only time actual products or services are launched or released to the public is after these have gone through a series of continuous improvements. That ensures no money or time was wasted in the actual production.

- The build-measure-learn system helps you see whether you should stick to the initial direction you planned to take or whether you should go on an entirely new direction. This is referred to as pivoting. Deciding when to pivot may be difficult, but if you don't want to fail in your endeavors, then you need to be open to the possibility of pivoting or turning to a new path.

- The lean startup approach is proven effective because of five principles that govern how it works. These same principles are what you need to apply in your business if you want it to succeed and especially when you apply the lean startup methodology.

- Accelerating the growth of your business is possible when you adopt the lean startup methodology.

- The lean startup method can also be used to efficiently manage your employees.

These are just some of the important points from this book. Hopefully, as you plan your business, the knowledge gleaned from this book can help you journey on the right path towards success. After all, that's the reason I came up with this book – to help you succeed by applying the lean startup methodology, just as I did.

Conclusion

I'd like to thank you and congratulate you for transiting my lines from start to finish.

I hope this book was able to help you to start a business that is destined to succeed from the very start. The purpose of this book is to reduce the number of failed businesses since these could have been prevented in the first place if only a system were in place.

The next step is to apply the proven steps to make your business succeed and grow around the lean startup methodology. Don't be another statistic. Be different from the rest. Work towards the success of your business by learning, adopting, and embracing the lean startup culture.

I wish you the best of luck!

Thank you

Before you go, I just wanted to say thank you for purchasing my book.

You could have picked from dozens of other books on the same topic but you took a chance and chose this one.

So, a HUGE thanks to you for getting this book and for reading all the way to the end.

Now I wanted to ask you for a small favor. ***Could you please consider posting a review on the platform? Reviews are one of the easiest ways to support the work of independent authors.***

This feedback will help me continue to write the type of books that will help you get the results you want. So if you enjoyed it, please let me know!

Click here to leave a review!

https://www.amazon.com/review/create-review/

References

Farbrot, A. (2014). Entrepreneurs Are More Single-Minded. Retrieved from https://partner.sciencenorway.no/bi-business-entrepreneurs/entrepreneurs-are-more-single-minded/1407583

Vojinovic, I. (2019). Thirty-Nine Entrepreneur Statistics You Need to Know in 2019. Retrieved from https://www.smallbizgenius.net/by-the-numbers/entrepreneur-statistics/

Entreprenoria. (2016). Top 10 Successful Entrepreneurs without a College Degree. Retrieved from https://entreprenoria.com/personal-development/top-10-successful-entrepreneurs-without-a-college-degree/

Price, R.W. (2011). What Is Entrepreneurial Management? Retrieved from https://news.gcase.org/2011/10/24/what-is-entrepreneurial-management/

Ries, E. (2011). The Roots of the Lean Startup. *The Lean Startup: How Today's Entrepreneurs Use Continuous Innovation to Create Radically Successful Businesses*, 28.

Pope, E. K. (2019). Startup vs. Small Business: What's the Difference? Retrieved from https://www.fundera.com/blog/startup-vs-small-business

McGowan, E. (2017). What Is Lean Startup Methodology – And How Can It Help You? Retrieved from https://www.startups.com/library/expert-advice/lean-startup-methodology-can-help

Expert Program Management. (2019). Book Summary: The Lean Startup by Eric Ries. Retrieved from https://expertprogrammanagement.com/2019/04/book-summary-lean-startup/

Peerbits. (2019) The Definitive Lean Startup Guide: Everything You Need to Know. Retrieved from

https://www.peerbits.com/blog/everythi
ng-you-need-know-about-lean-startup-
methodology.html

The Lean Startup. (n.d.). The Lean Startup
Methodology. Retrieved from
http://theleanstartup.com/principles

Ries, E. (2011). Batch. *The Lean Startup: How
Today's Entrepreneurs Use Continuous
Innovation to Create Radically
Successful Businesses*, 182.

Sheth, S (2019). Four Ways to Efficiently
Manage Employees in a Lean Startup.
Retrieved from
http://customerthink.com/4-ways-to-
efficiently-manage-employees-in-a-lean-
startup/

Ganti, A. (2019). Employee Stock Ownership
Plan (ESOP). Retrieved from

https://www.investopedia.com/terms/e/
esop.asp